Explode The Code® 2nd Edition 7

Essential lessons for phonics mastery

Nancy Hall • Rena Price

Do not feed
SPONGECAKE
The Elephant

EDUCATORS PUBLISHING SERVICE
Cambridge and Toronto

Cover art: Hugh Price

Text illustrations: Laura Price, Alan Price, Andrew Mockler, Meg Rosoff, Kelly Kennedy, Chris Vallo

Printed in Mayfield, PA, in May 2017
ISBN 978-0-8388-7807-1

3 4 5 PAH 19 18 17

CONTENTS

Lesson 1

When *c* is followed by *e*, *i*, or *y*, it usually says /s/, as in *ice*.

Circle the word that matches the picture.

1.	miss (mice) mince moss	2.	fast fact face force
3.	circus circle curling cereal	4.	dance dunce dice dunk
5.	dish disc decide dice	6.	coat sold cold cell
7.	slick slice splice sauce	8.	pecan palace pencil peace
9.	trace twice track ties	10.	justice juice icicle bounce

Circle the letters, and write the word that matches the picture.

1.		Spell.			Write.
		(d) b	un (an)	(ce) ct	_dance_
2.		j f	o a	ss ce	_____
3.		w m	i e	ce cle	_____
4.		l f	en em	co ce	_____
5.		spl sl	ai i	ce cle	_____
6.		g j	oa ui	ce cs	_____
7.		d p	i a	sh ce	_____

2

Join the syllables to make a word that fits each meaning.
Use your dictionary to help you.

1.	cir cle cus	An acrobat show <u>circus</u> A round, closed line <u>circle</u>
2.	test con cert	A race or test of skill _____ Musical entertainment _____
3.	ny cil pen	A one cent coin _____ Something to write or draw with _____
4.	sauce apple cider	Stewed apples _____ A drink made from apples _____ <div align="right">(two words)</div>
5.	force ful peace	Quiet and still _____ Full of power _____
6.	cess place re	To put back _____ A playtime between classes _____
7.	feat cide de	To make up your mind _____ To beat; to destroy _____

3

Yes or no?

	Yes	No
1. Have you ever seen sixteen dancing mice?	☐	☒
2. Do you sometimes have relay races during recess?	☐	☐
3. Can a thin pencil stand by itself in the center of a circle?	☐	☐
4. Would you like a slice of chocolate pound cake with your ice cream?	☐	☐
5. Will you dance the tango while you are taking a spelling test?	☐	☐
6. Would you like to wash your face with cold tomato juice?	☐	☐
7. Will you be twice as old on your next birthday as you are now?	☐	☐

Pick the best word to finish each sentence.

peaceful	cider	dancing
juicy	center	circle
~~pencil~~	circus	decide

1. When you do your homework, you need paper and
   a __pencil__ .

2. It is exciting to go to the _____ to see the lions
   and trapeze acts.

3. _____ is a great drink made from pressed apples.

4. Can you draw a _____ with a triangle in the middle?

5. When you grow up you will _____ what kind of
   job you want.

6. Peaches and tomatoes are very _____.

7. The pitcher stands in the _____ of the
   baseball diamond.

Put an X after the sentence that matches the picture.

1. Vance picked up the white mice and put them outside the white fence. ☐

   The white mice are singing and dancing on the picket fence. ☒

2. Grace gets a second chance to ride in the bicycle race. ☐

   Grace won second place in the important horse race. ☐

3. Nancy is scooping peaches and cream into the center of the shortcake. ☐

   Nancy decides to taste the big bucket of peach ice cream. ☐

4. Alice finds white mice racing on her new nightshirt. ☐

   Alice is dressed in a fancy new shirt with lace ruffles. ☐

5. Ms. Cellars gave the children juice and crackers at recess. ☐

   The children found juicy apples and crackers in the cellar. ☐

6. The split-rail fence kept the snorting bull from charging into the barnyard. ☐

   The split-rail fence encircles the barn and silo. ☐

7. Since Cindy could not go to the fancy dress ball, she decided to go to bed. ☐

   Cindy put on her fanciest gown to go dancing at the palace. ☐

6

Ella Cinders

Ella Cinders had a chance to go to a fancy ball at the royal palace. She wore a lovely long, blue lacy gown with a jewel necklace and a ruby red bracelet. Dressed up so splendidly, she looked like a real princess. The charming prince asked her twice to dance, but she would not. She decided she would rather relax, drink apple cider, and eat ice-cream sandwiches on the cool, breezy porch. It was too hot to dance, her face felt warm, her glass slippers were too tight, and she hated the slow music. Why didn't they play hip-hop?

Answer the following questions. You may look back at the story.

1. Where did Ella Cinders go? _____

    _____

2. What was her gown made of? _____

3. How many times did the prince ask her to dance? _____

4. What did she eat and drink? _____

    _____

5. Why did her feet hurt? _____

    _____

6. What kind of music did Ella like? _____

Using *c*, write the word that matches the picture. You may look back.

1.		<u>dance</u>
2.		_____
3.		_____
4.		_____
5.		_____
6.		_____
7.		_____

When *g* is followed by *e, i,* or *y,*
it sometimes says /j/, as in <u>gem</u> and *a<u>ge</u>.*

Circle the word that matches the picture.

1.		2.	
	cringe change cage crag		finger flipper fling fringe
3.	huge hug hung hook	4.	strange stage stag stooge
5.	hunger hanger hung hinge	6.	sprang spangle sprung sponge
7.	ladyfinger lady's slipper landlady ladybug	8.	pages paler package pageant
9.	bandit bangle bandage branding	10.	gerbil goodness garbage goose

Circle the letters, and write the word that matches the picture.

1.		Spell.					Write.
		h n	oi u	g ge			_____
2.		sk st	a e	ger ge			_____
3.		b p	u a	ges get			_____
4.		c cl	a o	ge gle			_____
5.		sp st	on or	g ge			_____
6.		j g	e i	n m			_____
7.		h n	in am	g ge			_____

Join the syllables to make a word that fits each meaning.
Use your dictionary to help you.

1.	age band pack	A large box or present _____ A piece of cloth that covers a wound or sore _____ _____
2.	gy stin spon	Not wanting to share or to spend money _____ Elastic and soft _____
3.	gen tur tle	Kind; tender; soft _____ A slow, crawling animal with a shell _____
4.	gin bil ger	A spicy seasoning _____ A small, mouselike pet_____
5.	able veget change	A plant that one eats _____ Likely to change _____
6.	teen post age	Stamps put on letters _____ Years between age thirteen and nineteen _____
7.	ble gin mar	A small, glass ball used in games_____ The space along the edge of a page _____

Yes or no?

	Yes	No
1. Can you keep a huge giraffe in a gold bird cage?	☐	☐
2. Would you like to change a rock into a gem?	☐	☐
3. If you get a strange package in the mail, do you get excited?	☐	☐
4. Does a small cottage have a stage in the cellar?	☐	☐
5. Will it help to use a big, plastic sponge as a bandage for a sore toe?	☐	☐
6. If the hinge of the door squeaks, will you grease it with ginger ale?	☐	☐
7. Can a gerbil read sixty pages in sixty days?	☐	☐

Pick the best word to finish each sentence.

luggage	sponge cake	postage
teenager	gerbil	stingy
gentleman	vegetables	changed

1. A _____ is a man with fine manners who is kind and helpful.

2. You must put _____ on all letters you send in the mail.

3. _____ with ice cream and caramel sauce is a wonderful dessert.

4. I have a pet _____ that I keep in a plastic cage.

5. We grow lots of green and yellow _____ in our garden.

6. Ella Cinders _____ her ragged dress before going to the fancy dress ball.

7. When you are a _____, you can learn to drive a car.

Put an X after the sentence that matches the picture.

1. The kind gentleman is carrying a sponge duck. ☐

   A sponge duck is carrying a kind gentleman. ☐

2. The gerbil is munching a ginger ice-cream cone. ☐

   The gerbil is crouching near the ice-cream stand. ☐

3. My teenage sister is pretending to be a queen on the stage. ☐

   Sixteen teenagers threw rotten oranges onto the stage. ☐

4. George wears a bandage on his forehead. ☐

   George fears his baggage was not forwarded. ☐

5. That certainly is a strange carriage with fringe on top. ☐

   The strange little cottage had fringed curtains in the windows. ☐

6. The hinges on the bird cage were pure gold, inlaid with gems. ☐

   Margy balanced a pure gold bird cage on her head. ☐

7. Rozita is changing into a space suit behind the stage. ☐

   Behind the stage is a strange spacecraft that Rozita constructed. ☐

A Gentle Joke

Gene and Marge were teenage twins. One hot day at the end of June, they were at their cottage by the lake. "Why don't you change into your swimsuits and walk to the lake?" said their mom. "Dad and I will join you later. We have to take the garbage to the town dump first."

When Gene and Marge got to the lake, they waved to Gerry the lifeguard and plunged right in. "Race you to the raft," Gene called. "OK," yelled Marge, "but what is that huge fish with giant orange fins doing on the raft?" "That's strange," called Gene, and he stopped swimming to look. "I don't see anything."

Marge was standing on the raft when she called back, "Made you look." When Gene joined Marge on the raft he winked and said, "You did, so now you owe me a ginger ice cream cone." Then he gave Marge a gentle push into the water and jumped in himself. "Race you to shore!" the twins shouted to each other.

Answer the following questions. You may look back at the story.

1. Why didn't their mom and dad walk to the lake with the twins?

   _____

2. How did Marge say the fish looked? _____

   _____

3. Who got to the raft first? _____

4. Was Gene mad at Marge? Why do you think so? _____

   _____

5. What kind of ice cream does Gene like? _____

15

Using *g*, write the word that matches the picture. You may look back.

1. _____

2. _____

3. _____

4. _____

5. _____

6. _____

7. _____

Lesson 3

Some words have silent letters.
When a word ends in *-dge*, the *d* is silent,
as in *bri<u>dge</u>*.

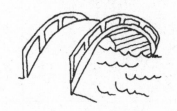

Circle the word that matches the picture.

1.		2.	
	budge		college
	baggy		etch
	dodge		edge
	badge		hedge

3.		4.	
	wedge		ridge
	ledge		doodle
	lodge		dozen
	long		dodge

5.		6.	
	brick		head
	bridge		hedge
	bride		hinge
	bring		hang

7.		8.	
	fudge		juggle
	fragrant		judge
	fungus		jungle
	nudge		grudge

9.		10.	
	badge		smudge
	bright		sledge
	bridge		smug
	bingo		snuggle

17

Circle the letters, and write the word that matches the picture.

		Spell.			Write.
1.		f fr	u o	dge de	_____
2.		t l	o a	g dge	_____
3.		br dr	u i	dg dge	_____
4.		e i		de dge	_____
5.		j g	u o	de dge	_____
6.		d b	e a	dge d	_____
7.		b sm	o u	dge dg	_____

Join the syllables to make a word that fits each meaning.
Use your dictionary to help you.

1.	gad bud get	A small useful tool _____ A plan for spending money _____
2.	mis judge take	An error or blunder _____ To think or decide unfairly_____
3.	fruit cake fudge	A heavy cake with fruit and nuts _____ A chocolate cake _____
4.	ger Dod bad	A member of a famous baseball team _____ A hairy, gray animal _____
5.	hammer sledge ing	Pounding nails into a board _____ A very large, heavy hammer_____
6.	gage hand bag	A woman's purse for carrying money _____ The bags of a traveler _____
7.	string bridge draw	A cord used to tighten sweatpants _____ A bridge that can be raised _____

Yes or no?

		Yes	No
1.	Can you wear a name badge on your shirt?	☐	☐
2.	Will you dodge the football if your teammate throws you a pass?	☐	☐
3.	Do you eat walnut fudge with your fingers and toes?	☐	☐
4.	If you were on the edge of a cliff, would you dance and tumble about?	☐	☐
5.	Can you use a bridge to cross the Atlantic Ocean?	☐	☐
6.	Do you hold a grudge if someone calls you a silly name?	☐	☐
7.	Would you use a sledgehammer to tack things onto a bulletin board?	☐	☐

Pick the best word to finish each sentence.

gadget	police badge	judge
dodge	hedge	lodger
edging	smudge	knowledge

1. Don't touch the walls when you clean the chimney; the black soot might leave a _____.

2. Use that _____ to open the bottle easily.

3. The _____ will decide the sentence after the jury gives the verdict.

4. The lovely purple bedspread is quilted and has an _____ of lavender lace.

5. Officer Slattery shows her _____ to prove she is an officer.

6. The soccer players _____ the opponents as they race to the goal.

7. When you clean up the yard, please mow the grass, weed the garden, and trim the tall, overgrown _____.

Put an X after the sentence that matches the picture.

1.	The tiny gentleman is stirring up fudge brownies. ☐	
	The little brownies danced cheerfully around the campfire. ☐	
2.	The judge ordered fudge cake and ice cream to go. ☐	
	The judge ordered the two teenagers to clean up the garbage. ☐	
3.	The bridge is carrying the traffic across the Mississippi River. ☐	
	The bride is marrying the groom with the big silver badge. ☐	
4.	The deep-sea diver is standing on the edge of the rocky ledge. ☐	
	The teenager is driving carefully along the edge of the rocky ledge. ☐	
5.	Jimmy's foot was lodged under the huge fallen goalpost. ☐	
	Jamal dodges a tackle and carries the football under the goalpost. ☐	
6.	The rustic lodge was constructed of huge logs and unfinished lumber. ☐	
	A new pick-up truck carries the rustic fence posts to the fortress. ☐	
7.	Midge practices swimming along the edge of the lake. ☐	
	Midge practices her dance steps near the edge of the stage. ☐	

22

The Tired Old Jeep

As Tomoko crossed the rickety bridge and started up the steep road over the mountain ridge, her old jeep began to sputter and spit. She drove several miles until the jeep finally stopped and would not budge. Tomoko leaped out and found she was standing on the edge of a rocky ledge. Looking down made her dizzy, but she took no notice. She pulled out her toolbox and crawled under the jeep to see if she could fix it. Then she discovered that one wheel was wedged between some rocks at the edge of the road. She could not get it free, even with four-wheel drive. What should she do now? Tomoko trudged up the road to hunt for a lodge to spend the night. She would have to return tomorrow with a tow truck.

Answer the following questions. You may look back at the story.

1. What did Tomoko drive across? _____

2. What kind of car did she have? _____

3. How did Tomoko feel? _____

4. Where was the wheel of the jeep stuck? _____

_____

5. What did Tomoko trudge up the road to find? _____

6. When would she return? _____

Using *dge*, write the word that matches the picture. You may look back.

1.		_____
2.		_____
3.		_____
4.		_____
5.		_____
6.		_____
7.		_____

Circle the word that matches the picture.

1.

city
silly
cent
citrus

2.

lace
large
latch
lark

3.

sprinkle
priceless
princess
principal

4.

bracelet
bracket
braces
branch

5.

angel
orange
arrange
organ

6.

giraffe
grant
giant
jungle

7.

sandwich
string
stage
strange

8.

passage
pencil
placed
palace

9.

rice
rash
race
erase

10.

ledge
pledge
plugs
page

Circle the letters, and write the word that matches the picture.

		Spell.				Write.
1.		n r	o a	ce ck		_____
2.		c k	i e	ty nt		_____
3.		dr pr	i in	ce ck		_____
4.		l f	ar or	ge g		_____
5.		or ar	an ai	ng ge		_____
6.		st str	in an	ge g		_____
7.		pl p	e ee	dge ge		_____

Join the syllables to make a word that fits each meaning.
Use your dictionary to help you.

1.	em let brace	Jewelry worn on the arm _____ To hug or hold in one's arms _____
2.	dan cer sau	One who dances _____ A small plate to set a cup on _____
3.	stran lar ger	Bigger _____ A person not known before _____
4.	cot tage advan	Having the odds in one's favor; having a good chance of winning _____ A small house or bungalow _____
5.	help price less	Very valuable _____ Not being able to help oneself _____
6.	cess re prin	The daughter of a king and queen _____ A playtime between classes _____
7.	i cing ra	Frosting on a cake _____ Running in a contest _____

Yes or no?

		Yes	No
1.	Do you face the American flag when you say the pledge?	☐	☐
2.	Could a fairy-tale princess live in a silver palace?	☐	☐
3.	If you were a stranger in a city, would you be lonely?	☐	☐
4.	Could a raccoon carry its baggage to the marketplace?	☐	☐
5.	Is it exciting to have relay races and dodgepball games at recess?	☐	☐
6.	Would you give a priceless bracelet to the grocer?	☐	☐
7.	Would a prince put on a lacy gown to go to a fancy dance?	☐	☐

Pick the best word to finish each sentence.

cottage	silence	unlace
excellent	grocery	stranger
enforce	passenger	exchange

1. If you wish to take off your sneakers, you must _____ them.

2. When you are baking shortcake and you run out of milk, you can go to the _____ store and buy a quart.

3. If you go to a new town where no one knows you, you are a _____.

4. A small house by a lake or pond is sometimes called a _____.

5. If you are traveling to Detroit on a train, you are a _____.

6. This pair of pants would fit a large gorilla! I'll take them back to the store and _____ them for my own size.

7. If you do a nearly perfect job on a paper, your teacher may tell you it is _____.

Put an X after the sentence that matches the picture.

1. Sara did not pay a large price for the fancy orange shirt. ☐

   Sara peeled large pieces of orange to share with her teenage pals. ☐

2. Sue has to exchange the new skirt she got on sale. ☐

   Sue and Jason are exchanging birthday gifts. ☐

3. The large savage beast emerged from the edge of the forest. ☐

   Francie embraced the large, furry Saint Bernard. ☐

4. Princess Lucy accepts the priceless pearl necklace. ☐

   Princess Lucy cares for nothing except her priceless horse, Prince. ☐

5. The brave general offered to help the downcast stranger. ☐

   The helpful general offered some water to the thirsty racer. ☐

6. Mario is in charge of mixing cement for the stone fireplace. ☐

   Mario is changing his socks beside the stone fireplace in the lodge. ☐

7. Everyone except Reggie entered the palace by the drawbridge. ☐

   The judge awarded Reggie first prize for winning the marathon race. ☐

30

Try the Fudge!

Reggie Cyrus is a candy maker. He is a genius when it comes to making smooth, ginger-flavored fudge. His success is due to six things:

1. He uses cream, not milk, in the fudge mixture.

2. He adds citrus peel, either lemon, orange, or lime.

3. He uses his own handmade device for mixing everything perfectly.

4. He does not stir the fudge mixture as it cooks.

5. He puts the fudge mixture in the refrigerator overnight.

6. He slices the fudge when it is ice cold.

Take my advice and have a gigantic piece of Reggie Cyrus's ginger-flavored fudge. It was judged by the Georgetown News to be Best in the City for five years in a row! And if you don't like ginger, try the chocolate or peanut butter fudge. Now you be the judge!

Find the word or words in the story that match each of the following meanings.

1. The opposite of failure _____

2. Huge _____

3. To decide what's good or bad _____

4. Citrus _____

5. A person who is very, very smart _____

6. A tool _____

In the crossword puzzle below, read each clue and write the word in the boxes. Remember that some words go across, and some words go down.

ACROSS

1. Peas grow inside this
3. A large town
5. A piece of cloth put on when one gets hurt
6. To shed tears
7. Opposite of west
9. A daughter of a king and queen
11. A place for inside athletic sports
12. A grand house for the ruler of an empire
13. A grain used in cereal
15. A super huge person
16. Soft, creamy candy

DOWN

1. To use toys
2. What someone does when playing dodgeball
3. Pet birds are kept in these
4. Opposite of no
5. Jewelry worn on the arm
8. A large striped animal of the cat family
9. To jump, dive, or throw oneself into the water
10. Ill; not well
12. Something that grows inside a pod
14. Frozen water

Lesson 5

Some words have silent letters.
When a word ends in *-mb*, the *b* is silent,
as in *comb*.

Look for the silent *b* in the words below.
Circle the word that matches the picture.

1.	cub cob comb camp	2.	limp limb lime list
3.	limb lamb lamp lab	4.	club crank crumb crowd
5.	crime club cling climb	6.	them tumble thumb thump
7.	crumb crook cram crab	8.	comb cob cone climb
9.	plum plumb plate plot	10.	thimble thumbnail dumbbell thumbtack

Circle the letters, and write the word that matches the picture. Remember the silent *b*.

		Spell.			Write.
1.		m l	i a	b mb	_____
2.		g c	o a	mb b	_____
3.		th t	o u	me mb	_____
4.		n l	e i	mb mp	_____
5.		cl ch	i u	nb mb	_____
6.		gr cr	u a	mb mp	_____
7.		d c	e omb	ing b	_____

Join the syllables to make a word that fits each meaning.
Use your dictionary to help you.

1.
trem	To shake with fear _____
ble	To break into small bits _____
crum	

2.
comb	Smoothing the hair _____
honey	The place where bees store honey _____
ing	

3.
chop	A meat to eat for supper _____ _____
lamb	You might eat Chinese food with (two words)
sticks	these _____

4.
bell	A lovely flower_____
dumb	A heavy weight used for exercise _____
blue	

5.
thumb	The hard covering of one finger_____
tack	A pin used to attach things to a bulletin board
nail	_____

6.
shell	The outer part of a nut_____
bomb	A shattering upset; a surprise _____
nut	

7.
cite	To stir up feelings_____
ex	To repeat aloud _____
re	

Yes or no?

		Yes	No
1.	Can a curly gray lamb comb its hair?	☐	☐
2.	Can a gigantic tiger climb out on the end of a limb?	☐	☐
3.	When you eat a toasted sandwich, do you sometimes get crumbs on your shirt?	☐	☐
4.	Have you ever stuck your thumb in a coconut whipped-cream pie?	☐	☐
5.	Would it be dumb to lock your keys inside your car?	☐	☐
6.	Does the plumber who comes to fix the kitchen sink bring a basket of plums?	☐	☐
7.	Do you use a lamb chop to chop down a maple tree?	☐	☐

Pick the best word to finish each sentence.

climbing	lamb chops	combing
thumbnail	plumber	tumbling
crumbling	crumb cake	beachcomber

1. The _____ fixes the pipes when they are leaking.

2. The fire fighter is _____ up the ladder to the roof where the fire is burning.

3. The judge has ordered broiled _____ with mashed potatoes for dinner.

4. It is best to use a nail clipper to trim your _____.

5. A _____ walks along the beach picking up seashells.

6. The teenager is _____ the long-haired cat to get the tangles out of its fur.

7. For breakfast we sometimes bake a _____, which is really good to eat when it is still warm.

Put an X after the sentence that matches the picture.

1. Tess uses all her strength to push the thumbtack into the plaster wall. ☐

   Tess stretches the elastic belt between her thumbs. ☐

2. Margy dipped the lamb chop in bread crumbs. ☐

   The lamb chop threw bread crumbs at Margy. ☐

3. Lizzy painted her thumbnails with light purple nail polish. ☐

   The painter held the lizard between his thumbs. ☐

4. Here are some lamb chops for the hungry tiger. ☐

   The man is trying to lift the heavy dumbbell. ☐

5. Rudy is brushing and combing his long dark curls. ☐

   Rudy is brushing and combing his lanky polo pony. ☐

6. Donna crumbled the cookie all over the doll house. ☐

   The cookie crumbs made Kate's car seat a mess. ☐

7. The girl spilled the box of thumbtacks. ☐

   Her thumbnails were painted with flowers. ☐

The Lamb and the Plumber

One hot September morning, Lucky Lamb sat with a comb in front of the mirror trying to untangle all that matted hair. Suddenly the doorbell rang. It was Paula, the plumber, who had come to fix the leaky pipes in the bathroom. She was hot and out of breath. She had had to climb all the way up to Lucky's apartment on the tenth floor since the elevator was not working. After she arrived, she discovered that she needed a different tool from her plumber's truck. Annoyed, she stomped out of the apartment. On the way out she tripped on a dumbbell and hurt her thumb. "Ouch," she muttered. The curly lamb just said, "Baaaa."

Answer the following questions. You may look back at the story.

1. What was Lucky Lamb holding? _____

2. Who rang the doorbell? _____

3. Why had the plumber come? _____

_____

4. How had she gotten to the tenth floor? _____

_____

5. What did she trip on? _____

_____

6. What did the lamb say? _____

39

Using -mb, write the word that matches the picture. You may look back.

1.	_____
2.	_____
3.	_____
4.	_____
5.	_____
6.	_____
7.	_____

Lesson 6

Some words have silent letters.
When a word begins with *kn,* the *k* is silent,
as in <u>k</u>nife.

Look for the silent *k* in the words below.
Circle the word that matches the picture.

1.
knit
knight
known
knockout

2.
keep
knee
knew
knead

3.
crock
knock
knack
knobby

4.
knothole
knowledge
picnic
pickax

5.
knew
neck
knapsack
kneel

6.
knave
knock
knot
know

7.
nickel
knuckle
nickname
knickers

8.
knight
kite
knife
kickoff

9.
kite
kit
knit
night

10.
know
ketchup
knot
knob

Circle the letters, and write the word that matches the picture.

#		Spell.			Write.
1.		kn k	ee a	l t	_____
2.		gn kn	e i	lt t	_____
3.		kn sn	o u	ke ck	_____
4.		kn k	u o	be b	_____
5.		hn kn	i igh	t st	_____
6.		kn k	ou o	b t	_____
7.		kn gn	ai i	v fe	_____

Join the syllables to make a word that fits each meaning.
Use your dictionary to help you.

1.	size knee cap	To turn over; to become overturned _____ The bone that protects the front of the knee _____ _____
2.	knick knack ers	A small object or ornament _____ Baggy knee-length pants _____
3.	nick name el	What your friends call you _____ A 5 cent coin _____
4.	er out knock	What you do to win at boxing _____ A handle found on a door and used for knocking _____
5.	knot hole ted	A hole in a board _____ Full of knots _____
6.	knap ful sack	Enough to fill a bag _____ A canvas bag worn on the back _____
7.	knuc sprin kle	Light drops of rain _____ A joint in a finger _____

Yes or no?

	Yes	No
1. Can you knock on a closed door with your knuckles?	☐	☐
2. Does a brave knight know how to fight a dragon?	☐	☐
3. Can a lamb knit purple knee socks?	☐	☐
4. Will a snow bunny put on knickers when it is skating?	☐	☐
5. Would you kneel in the grass to look for a lost nickel?	☐	☐
6. Can a desk have knobs for handles?	☐	☐
7. Does a giraffe know how to untie a knot?	☐	☐

Pick the best word to finish each sentence.

doorknob	know-how	knee-deep
knife	knee socks	knitted
knapsack	knots	knuckle

1. Carmen filled her _____ with all the supplies she would need for the camping trip.

2. Valencia wore a blouse, a pleated skirt, and blue _____ with sneakers to the party.

3. Since the door sticks, you must turn the _____ and pull very hard.

4. Shawn has the _____ to fix anything that needs repairing.

5. A passenger on the bus _____ a soft cashmere sweater to help pass the time on the long trip.

6. Tie the boat to the dock with strong _____ and remember to tighten them.

7. When you go fishing, be sure to take your boots because you will be _____ in water.

Put an X after the sentence that matches the picture.

1. The noble knight rode bravely into battle. ☐

   The nearsighted knight will drive into a bottle. ☐

2. The truck driver is kneeling to change the tire. ☐

   The truck driver is knee-deep in the flowers. ☐

3. Noel needed a knife to cut the cake. ☐

   Noel's knee banged into the cake. ☐

4. Trish's cat knocked over the empty trash barrels. ☐

   Trish's hat was knocked off by an icy snowball. ☐

5. Cindy knitted new striped knee socks for Yusef. ☐

   Yusef has checkered knee socks that match his new knickers. ☐

6. Joyce's knees begin to quake when she must travel by plane. ☐

   Joyce knows that she needs to take her luggage on the airplane. ☐

7. Randy's knees shake as he rings the doorbell on his first date. ☐

   Randy scraped his knuckles on the rusty hinge of the gate. ☐

Knute the Robot

Knute was a robot that worked at Cindy's Camping Supplies. The store sold things like knapsacks, folding knives, and knitted hiking socks. It also sold tents, which Knute put up in the store so customers knew what they looked like. Knute could put up a tent twice as fast as a human!

But one morning Cindy saw Knute working very slowly and stiffly. He failed to knot the ropes. He couldn't prop up the poles to raise the tent. She knew he had a problem. He couldn't bend, lift, or even kneel!

Cindy looked up the problem in her *Know Your Robot* book. Then she climbed up, opened Knute's control panel, and pressed some buttons. Slowly but surely, Knute began to bend his knees and crack his knuckles. And just in time. There were customers knocking on the door and rattling the doorknob. "Back to work, Knute," Cindy said.

Answer the following questions. You may look back at the story.

1. Name two things that were sold at Cindy's store. _____

    _____

2. What was Knute's job? _____

3. How did Cindy know that Knute had a problem? _____

    _____

4. What did Cindy do to fix the problem? _____

    _____

5. Why was it important for Cindy to fix Knute right away? _____

    _____

Using the silent *k*, write the word that matches the picture. You may look back.

1. _____

2. _____

3. _____

4. _____

5. _____

6. _____

7. _____

Lesson 7

Some words have silent letters.
When a word begins with *wr*, the *w* is silent,
as in _wreath_.

Look for the silent *w* in the words below.
Circle the word that matches the picture.

1. white / write / which / wring	**2.** report / wrap / wrong / wreck
3. wrinkle / wrens / rinse / rent	**4.** weak / writing / repeat / wreck
5. ranch / wren / wrench / which	**6.** warble / rescue / wrestle / wrinkles
7. worth / wreath / wealth / watch	**8.** reptile / wrist / resting / rustle
9. wrist / whistle / western / written	**10.** rung / wring / wiggle / wrong

Circle the letters, and write the word that matches the picture.

		Spell.			Write.
1.		w wr	e i	nt st	_____
2.		wr mr	o u	nb ng	_____
3.		wr br	a i	te t	_____
4.		sr wr	ea ai	sh th	_____
5.		wr w	oi i	ng mp	_____
6.		wr cr	a u	p b	_____
7.		w wr	ee en	ch th	_____

50

Join the syllables to make a word that fits each meaning.
Use your dictionary to help you.

1.

| age
wreck
voy | A long trip by sea or air _____

The remains of a crash _____ |

2.

| wrap
whis
per | To speak softly _____

A covering for gum _____ |

3.

| twin
kle
wrin | A crease or fold in a person's skin _____

To shine like a star _____ |

4.

| wrist
dog
watch | A small clock worn on the arm _____

A dog used to protect a home _____ |

5.

| ship
ment
wreck | The wreckage of a large boat _____

Goods that are shipped _____ |

6.

| writing
kerchief
hand | Writing done by hand _____

A soft cloth used to wipe the nose or face

_____ |

7.

| ten
writ
nis | A game played with a racket, ball, and net

_____

Put into writing _____ |

Yes or no?

	Yes	No
1. Can a metal wrench wriggle like a rattlesnake?	☐	☐
2. Would you like to be a successful writer someday?	☐	☐
3. Does a wristwatch sometimes tell the wrong time?	☐	☐
4. Can a little wren write its nickname in script?	☐	☐
5. Would you wrap crisp lettuce in birthday paper?	☐	☐
6. Can you hold a gum wrapper in your hand?	☐	☐
7. If you wreck your bicycle, will you be upset?	☐	☐

Pick the best word to finish each sentence.

shipwrecked	handwriting	wrinkled
wristband	wrongdoing	wrestle
written	wrapped	wrathful

1. The teacher says that Pat has very nice _____.

2. After sitting up all night on the train, the passenger's pants were very _____.

3. Have you _____ a thank-you note to your grandmother?

4. When the power went out in the grocery store, no one was blamed for any _____.

5. During the storm, the ship was cast up on the rocks and was _____.

6. The shopkeeper _____ the present in bright ribbons andcolorful paper.

7. On his right arm he always wore a braided _____ made of rope.

Put an X after the sentence that matches the picture.

1. There was a shipwreck during last night's storm. ☐

   The goofy knight will wreck his armor in the bathtub. ☐

2. The plumber is using a giant wrench to repair the plumbing. ☐

   The wren is pecking at the gigantic plums on the tree. ☐

3. Paula is concerned because she got the wrong paper. ☐

   Paula played several wrong notes at the concert. ☐

4. Jacky is writing a letter to the newly-elected president. ☐

   Jacky is dragging away the smashed cars with the wrecker. ☐

5. The wreath is made of holly, ropes of ivy, and red ribbon. ☐

   Holly wrenched her knee while skipping jump rope. ☐

6. Sondra wrapped her spotted cat in a blanket. ☐

   Sondra skidded on ice and wrecked her car on the pole. ☐

7. The gold wristband was found in the wren's nest. ☐

   The well-known writer was presented with a large gold wristwatch. ☐

54

The Bike Wreck

Norma spent all her money on a brand new ten-speed racing bike. She went down the street to show her pals. They were playing marbles when she rode up, and she had to flip a wheelie to get them to look up at her new bike. Unluckily, as the bike tipped back, the handlebars turned the wrong way, and Norma ran right into a brick wall. She was thrown off and landed on her wrist and broke it. Her new bike was a tangled wreck. Norma's wrist was put in a cast and wrapped in a sling for seven weeks. During this time she could not write or do her homework. Poor Norma! When she recovered, she tried to repair the bent bike frame with a hammer and wrench, but it still had a wrinkled fender and now it looked like an old, beat-up bike.

Answer the following questions. You may look back at the story.

1. What did Norma purchase with her money? _____

    _____

2. What did she do to get her pals to look up? _____

    _____

3. What was broken? _____

    _____

4. What was Norma unable to do for seven weeks? _____

    _____

5. What tools did Norma use to fix the bent frame? _____

    _____

6. How did the fender look when she finished? _____

Using the silent *w*, write the word that matches the picture. You may look back.

1.		_____
2.		_____
3.		_____
4.		_____
5.		_____
6.		_____
7.		_____

Lesson 8

Sometimes the letter *t* is silent when it comes in the middle of a word, as in *whis<u>t</u>le*.

Look for the silent *t* in the words below.
Circle the word that matches the picture.

1.
cast
cattle
castle
circus

2.
feast
forest
faster
fasten

3.
whistle
whirlpool
wishful
whisker

4.
luster
liver
listen
litter

5.
wheelbarrow
whistle
wretched
wreckage

6.
glimpse
glisten
gristle
ginger

7.
gristle
grizzly
gritty
grassy

8.
thistle
thicken
thirst
thither

9.
soften
shorten
sorting
Scottish

10.
bridge
brittle
British
bristle

Circle the letters, and write the word that matches the picture.

1.		Spell.				Write.
		wh sh	as is	te tle		_____
2.		f l	is es	ten net		_____
3.		c ch	as a	tle ten		_____
4.		c s	of if	ten fed		_____
5.		wh gr	es is	tle ser		_____
6.		f p	as o	ten ter		_____
7.		g gl	is i	ten ned		_____

58

Join the syllables to make a word that fits each meaning.
Use your dictionary to help you.

1.	tler whis wres	A person who takes part in a match _____ A person who makes a shrill sound with the lips _____
2.	has lis ten	To try to hear _____ To hurry; to go fast _____
3.	of fas ten	Many times; frequently _____ To attach together _____
4.	tle bris gris	Short, stiff hair, as on a brush _____ A piece of fiber that makes meat hard to chew _____
5.	ten sof glis	To make soft _____ To shine; to sparkle _____
6.	castle wich sand	Towers and walls made of sand _____ Two slices of bread with filling between them _____
7.	this whis tle	A high, shrill sound _____ A prickly plant _____

Yes or no?

		Yes	No
1.	Do you like gristle in your sirloin steak?	☐	☐
2.	Do you think a knight might have lived in a splendid castle?	☐	☐
3.	Is it pleasant to listen to the wind rustle the trees?	☐	☐
4.	Can a gold necklace have a clasp to fasten it together?	☐	☐
5.	Can a broiled lamb chop whistle "Yankee Doodle"?	☐	☐
6.	Will charcoal soften your skin and brighten your teeth?	☐	☐
7.	Do you chew the stiff bristles of your toothbrush?	☐	☐

Pick the best word to finish each sentence.

listen	rustle	wrestled
hastens	whistling	gristle
fastener	often	bristles

1. This hairbrush has stiff _____.

2. Lionel _____ to class when he hears the bell ring.

3. If you do something frequently, you do it _____.

4. Wen Li likes to _____ to her music.

5. The song of some birds sounds like _____.

6. Suddenly there was a _____ of leaves as a rabbit scooted into the woods.

7. The teammates tumbled and rolled on the ground as they _____ one another.

Put an X after the sentence that matches the picture.

1. Ivan listened to the brass trumpet quartet in the concert hall. ☐

   Roger connected the electric wire to the outside lantern. ☐

2. Ellie May has a golden retriever that can whistle tunes. ☐

   Ellie May whistled for her golden retriever, Max. ☐

3. The king of Sweden chooses a new throne for his castle. ☐

   The doorknob on the castle glistens in the sunlight. ☐

4. The wrestlers are resting and swinging in the hammocks. ☐

   Wrestlers are often very strong and muscular. ☐

5. Melissa is going to use a bristly brush to paint the fence. ☐

   Matthew softens his bristly beard with shaving cream. ☐

6. Mary Jo fastens the ropes on the giant clipper ship. ☐

   Rosemary needs a giant paper clip as a fastener. ☐

7. By mistake, Kevin puts hand softener on his waffles. ☐

   Foolish Kevin hangs his large rubber boots by the fire to warm them. ☐

Madge Visits Whistler Castle

Madge was on a class trip to the Whistler Castle Museum. The first thing Madge saw inside the museum was a knight's suit of armor. She often read about the kings, queens, and knights who lived in castles. So when she saw the armor, she began to imagine castle life long ago.

Madge imagined the sounds and sights. She listened to the rustling of the queen's skirts, the king's whistling for his hounds, and the knight's armor clanking as he climbed upon his horse. She saw the bristles of a brush as a lady-in-waiting brushed the queen's hair until it softened and glistened. She saw two knights unfasten their armor and wrestle to entertain the king.

But then Madge had to leave her castle dream. Her teacher was calling, and Madge hastened to join her class in the museum gift shop.

Answer the following questions. You may look back at the story.

1. Where was the museum located? _____

2. What did Madge begin to imagine when she first saw the knight's

   armor? _____

3. What was one sound that Madge imagined? One sight? _____

   _____

4. Who called for Madge? Why? _____

   _____

5. What does the word *hastened* mean? _____

   _____

Using the silent *t*, write the word that matches the picture. You may look back.

1. _____

2. _____

3. _____

4. _____

5. _____

6. _____

7. _____

Lesson 9

In some words, the letter *h* is silent, as in *rhythm*.

Look for the silent *h* in the words below.
Circle the word that matches the picture.

1.	how hour hair hoe	**2.**	regular rhubarb pie pineapple runaway
3.	hoofbeat honey honest hornet	**4.**	ripple rhinoceros rhinestone rickshaw
5.	jog joke join John	**6.**	rhino rhythm rhombus rude
7.	her herb herd hurt	**8.**	shepherd shipped seldom sherbet
9.	Rhonda rhubarb rhino rollerskate	**10.**	household horsehair hourglass homeless

65

Circle the letters, and write the word that matches the picture.

1.		Spell.				Write.
		shep	sheep	herd	harb	_____
2.						
		ma	mo	tel	let	_____
3.						
		rhy	hu	sp	thm	_____
4.						
		hon	hen	less	or	_____
5.						
		hon	hour	lisp	glass	_____
6.						
		tea	sea	cup	cub	_____
7.						
		ri	rhi	toe	no	_____

Join the syllables to make a word that fits each meaning.
Use your dictionary to help you.

1.
barb	A person who cuts hair _____
rhu	A garden plant whose stalks are used in pies and
er	sauce _____

2.
ly	
hour	Truthfully _____
honest	Happening every hour _____

3.
glass	
hour	The total amount held in a glass _____
ful	A device for measuring time _____

4.
hibit	
ex	To tire out_____
haust	To show publicly _____

5.
or	
hon	A person who acts on a stage_____
act	Praise; respect_____

6.
grit	
hones	Full of sand _____
ty	Telling the truth _____

7.
al	
herb	Made of herbs _____
gener	A high-ranking officer in the army_____

Yes or no?

		Yes	No
1.	Does a rhinoceros have birthday parties?	☐	☐
2.	Do you live in an apartment in Rhode Island?	☐	☐
3.	Can you tell time with an hourglass?	☐	☐
4.	Do you like peppermint herbal tea?	☐	☐
5.	Would you be exhausted if you jogged five miles?	☐	☐
6.	Are you on your honor always to tell the truth?	☐	☐
7.	Would it be ghastly to shake hands with a gorilla?	☐	☐

Pick the best word to finish each sentence.

honor	honesty	hour
herbs	shepherds	exhausted
exhibit	ghastly	rhubarb

1.

Gina went to the art show to see Rhett's art _____.

2.

After running all the way to the post office and back again,
Teeshan is _____.

3.

Grandmother enjoys picking chives, dill, and other
_____ to put in her fresh garden salad.

4.

It is an _____ to have the president sit at the
head of our table.

5.

The _____ searched for the lost lambs because
a wolf was nearby.

6.

Do not tell lies; _____ is the best policy.

7.

The little bird comes out of the cuckoo clock every
_____.

Put an X after the sentence that matches the picture.

1. They timed the race with a small hourglass. ☐

   They had toast and jam for breakfast. ☐

2. Thomas has a ghastly new polka-dotted necktie. ☐

   The gorilla gives Thomas a gentle hug. ☐

3. Ginger helps the author rewrite the book. ☐

   George was honest about chopping down the cherry tree. ☐

4. The shepherd lost his flock of sheep during the night. ☐

   The flock of gulls attacked the shellfish on the beach. ☐

5. Francie grows rhubarb and parsley in her herb garden. ☐

   Francie sets a hot rhubarb pie on the window sill. ☐

6. Loren is aghast when she sees the hour is midnight. ☐

   Loren stands beside the huge hourglass. ☐

7. The rodent is exhausted from rolling in the dirt. ☐

   The rhino is extremely well hidden in the slimy pool. ☐

Dinner in the Jungle

General Rhodes lived in the jungle with his two pets, a white German Shepherd named Ghostly and a baby rhino named Rhonda. The General worked hard for many hours every day gathering facts about wildlife. He was often so exhausted at the end of the day that making dinner was a chore. So he would pick some fruit from the trees and some rhubarb and herbs from his garden for a fast and easy meal. He and his pets ate it because they were hungry, not because it tasted that good!

After one of his endless workdays, General Rhodes returned to the campsite and was aghast to find his pets gone! Then he smelled something wonderful and followed his nose to the next campsite. It was there that General Rhodes found his friend Cyd feeding his pets.

"Honestly, Cyd," he said. "I don't blame them."

"Please, pull up a stool," said Cyd, exhibiting her best manners. Then she spooned some yummy stew into bowls for her friends.

Answer the following questions. You may look back at the story.

1. Where did General Rhodes live? Why? _____

   _____

2. What kind of pets did General Rhodes have? _____

3. What does the word *aghast* mean? _____

4. What did the General find at Cyd's campsite? _____

   _____

5. Why didn't the General blame his pets for going there? _____

   _____

Using the silent *h*, write the word that matches the picture. You may look back.

1. _____

2. _____

3. _____

4. _____

5. _____

6. _____

7. _____

Lesson 10 • Review Lesson

Remember, some words have silent letters.

Circle the word that matches the picture.

1.
hollyhock
honeysuckle
honeymoon
honeycomb

2.
houseboat
horsefly
ransack
racehorse

3.
rhythm
rhino
rhubarb
rhyme

4.
knickknack
knee socks
knighthood
kneading

5.
casserole
chasing
castle
circle

6.
warehouse
wren house
White House
worthy

7.
lumber
clobber
clearing
climber

8.
whittling
whistling
wrestling
whirlpool

9.
waistband
wristwatch
weekend
wreckage

10.
knothole
kickoff
knocker
know-how

Circle the letters, and write the word that matches the picture.

		Spell.					Write.
1.		rh ph	y e	thm sp			_____
2.		k kn	ee ew				_____
3.		w wr	a o	nt te			_____
4.		wr w	e i	rk ck			_____
5.		c g	as os	tle ty			_____
6.		kn k	a o	ck ch			_____
7.		c cl	i u	b mb			_____

74

Join the syllables to make a word that fits each meaning.
Use your dictionary to help you.

1.	knock cast out	Alone and friendless _____ To put a player out of a game _____
2.	hole knot cubby	A small place to keep your things _____ A hole in a board where a knot has fallen out _____
3.	comb moon honey	A wax form made by bees _____ A holiday trip taken by a bride and groom _____
4.	cap size knee	The bone which protects the front of the knee _____ To upset; to overturn _____
5.	ted knit spot	Made of yarn by means of long needles _____ Stained with dots or specks _____
6.	knob bell door	A door buzzer or chime to be rung _____ A handle used to open a door _____
7.	hand coach stage	A horse-drawn covered wagon used to carry passengers and mail _____ A worker who handles lights, props, and sets in a play _____

75

Yes or no?

	Yes	No
1. Would you be able to knock down the boxing champ?	☐	☐
2. Could a pigeon fly through a knothole?	☐	☐
3. Would a shepherd need knee socks to keep warm in bed?	☐	☐
4. Are mountain climbers exhausted when they reach the peak?	☐	☐
5. Could you tell the time if you had a new wristwatch?	☐	☐
6. Would you need a hat with netting to get near the honeycomb in a beehive?	☐	☐
7. Does your house look like a knight's castle?	☐	☐

Pick the best word to finish each sentence.

knives	knothole	castle
honeycomb	wallet	knee socks
wreckage	climbing	rhubarb

1. With her shovel and pail, Ginny is constructing a huge sand _____ on the beach.

2. The family cleaned up the _____ after the storm.

3. While you are _____ a mountain, you may get very thirsty and tired.

4. A strawberry and _____ pie was delicious!

5. When you set the table for dinner, you put on forks, _____, and spoons.

6. I wrote my name and address in my _____, so if it is lost, someone will be able to return my money.

7. Averill always puts on _____ with her sneakers.

Put an X after the sentence that matches the picture.

1. Hans coasted on the snowy slope until his feet were numb. ☐

   The sports car went so smoothly that Chan coasted along the road. ☐

2. The best honey comes right in its own honeycomb. ☐

   Jasmine is combing her long honey-colored hair. ☐

3. The knight in shining armor won the fierce duel. ☐

   The knight in shining armor was cut on the arm in the fierce duel. ☐

4. Hilary is whistling for her colt to come over to the wall. ☐

   Hilary's colt leaps over the wall and gallops off at a fast pace. ☐

5. Herbie got an honor award for his honesty and good citizenship. ☐

   Herbie was a dishonest citizen because he stole a wallet. ☐

6. The tiny wren rattles around in the house after the nestlings have flown away. ☐

   The rattlesnake is trying to climb into the tiny wren house. ☐

7. Thomas tries to see the game by peeking through the knothole. ☐

   Thomas knows he has a great seat to watch the baseball game. ☐

Midnight Visitors

The Conway family had pitched a tent in a woodsy campground in Vermont. They roasted hamburgers and corn on the cob for supper. Afterward, everyone pitched in with the clean-up so they could go to bed early. Wrapped in their sleeping bags, they had just fallen asleep when they were awakened by a crash. The garbage can had been knocked over. They must have forgotten to fasten the lid!

Marie looked at her wristwatch. The hour was late. It was half-past eleven. She grabbed her flashlight and ran to see who the raider was. Marie knelt down and peeked around the tent. Five fat raccoons stuck their heads out of the trash can. They had been wrestling inside the can for scraps, and their faces were covered with crumbs. Quickly they climbed out of the barrel and scampered up a nearby tree, peering down as if to ask, "Is it wrong to like corn on the cob?"

Find the word in the story that matches each of the following meanings.

1. Covered-up by winding or folding something around _____

2. To hold together; to make secure _____

3. The time of day or night _____

4. Struggling or fighting to get control _____

5. Bits of food _____

6. Went up by using both hands and feet _____

In the crossword puzzle below, read each clue and write the word in the boxes.
Remember that some words go across, and some words go down.

ACROSS

1. A brave man who in ancient times wore a metal suit
4. Truthful
6. The liquid of a fruit
7. A platform where plays are held
8. The referee blows this to stop a game
12. The name of a color and a fruit
13. Hidden or secret power
14. A large, important town
16. A circular shape made of flowers or leaves
18. A hole in a board where a knot has come out
20. A baby sheep
21. To destroy
22. A sheriff wears one of these on a uniform

DOWN

2. Frozen water
3. A prickly plant, the name of which sounds like *whistle*
5. A bird lays this
9. A wax form made by bees to hold honey
10. A small clock worn on the arm
11. A person who races
15. A liquid used in a pen
16. A tool used to turn nuts and bolts
17. Sixty minutes make one _____
19. To go up or down by using both hands and feet, as on a ladder

Lesson 11

Sometimes *ear* says /air/, as in *bear*.

Circle the word that matches the picture.

1.
peacock
pantry
pear tree
partridge

2.
vegetable
valley
volleyball
video

3.
underworld
underwater
underneath
outerwear

4.
tear
tar
term
tire

5.
snickers
speakers
sneakers
sweater

6.
smokestack
smoking
Smokey the Bear
smoothest

7.
sweet
swarm
swear
smear

8.
perfume
pear-shaped
perhaps
polar bear

9.
football
footwear
footstool
footprint

10.
wearing
warring
weekday
weather

Circle the letters, and write the word that matches the picture.

1.		Spell.			Write.
		p b	i ea	n r	_____
2.		sl cl	e	a m p	_____
3.		sw s	eat ear	belt dell	_____
4.		d b	ee ea	p r	_____
5.		l tr	a ea	d p	_____
6.		w h	ea a	ck r	_____
7.		tr t	ea a	r m	_____

Join the syllables to make a word that fits each meaning.
Use your dictionary to help you.

1.	wear space outer	Where astronauts go _____ Heavier clothing worn over one's clothing _____
2.	shaped mis pear-	Badly shaped _____ In the form of a pear _____
3.	able suit bear	Fitting; right for the time _____ Not too much discomfort or pain for a person to stand _____
4.	wreck swear ing	Promising to do something _____ Destroying _____
5.	stool wear foot	That which is worn on the feet _____ A place to rest the feet _____
6.	ing squirt tear	Spraying a liquid, like water _____ Pulling apart; ripping _____
7.	black bill board	Something you write on with chalk _____ A large roadside advertisement _____

Yes or no?

		Yes	No
1.	Would you be afraid of falling if you skated with a grumpy bear?	☐	☐
2.	Do you wear a helmet when you ride your bike?	☐	☐
3.	Can wild pears grow on an old apple tree?	☐	☐
4.	Is there a day each season when grizzly bears talk to each other?	☐	☐
5.	Will we hang all the clean wash-and-wear clothing out to dry?	☐	☐
6.	Would a robin wear large earrings to a wedding?	☐	☐
7.	Can you talk to a pear-shaped bear sitting in a bathtub?	☐	☐

Pick the best word to finish each sentence.

seat belt	pear-shaped	outerwear
wash-and-wear	Smokey the Bear	cream puff
swearing	leaking	tearing

1. The basement is filling up with water because the pipes are
   _____.

2. Clothes that are made of _____ fabric dry quickly.

3. _____ tells us to be careful with matches and to
   help prevent forest fires.

4. A _____ is big and yummy to eat.

5. When you go skating, you must be sure to wear your warm
   _____.

6. When you are riding in a car, it is important to wear a
   _____.

7. Jon is upset because the teacher wrote "poor" on his messy
   paper; now he is _____ the paper up.

Put an X after the sentence that matches the picture.

1. The hungry teenager tears the grilled steak apart. ☐

   The teenager swears he will get on the honor roll next term. ☐

2. It will take teamwork to get all the pears picked before it snows. ☐

   Our teammate is stepping over the small pear tree. ☐

3. Rock climbing is wearing out the knees of Mark's blue jeans. ☐

   Marcus tears his knee socks while climbing into the rocket ship. ☐

4. The old bear tears at the hive. ☐

   The old crow throws pears at the bell hanging in the steeple. ☐

5. Ruby cannot bear wearing silk stockings. ☐

   The bear is wearing ruby beads and gold earrings. ☐

6. Kendra sprained her wrist on New Year's Eve. ☐

   Kendra has a broken leg on New Year's Day. ☐

7. Jocko is feasting on pumpkin pie with whipped cream. ☐

   The jack-o'-lantern is having a whipped-cream shampoo. ☐

Larry Bear's Pear Surprise

Larry was a huge bear. His favorite appliance was a well-stocked refrigerator. If it happened to have ice cream, pears, and chocolate syrup in it, all the better. Then he would make his favorite dessert—Larry Bear's Pear Surprise. He liked to make it when his friends came over and often just for himself!

One year Larry ate far too many desserts, and he could not touch his toes even if he bent his knees. He liked to wear nice things, but lately all of his nice things were tearing and their buttons were popping off.

So Larry made a pledge. "I swear that I'll take off some pounds this year," he told himself. "I'll reduce by being careful about what I eat. I'll go from huge to just plain large, as a bear should be. And when I get there, I'll splurge on a Pear Surprise with my friends!"

And that's just what Larry did.

Answer the following questions. You may look back at the story.

1. What was Larry's favorite dessert? _____

2. Who did he make it for? _____

   _____

3. One year, Larry had a problem. What was it? _____

4. What did Larry decide to do about his problem? _____

   _____

5. Was Larry's plan a success? _____

   _____

Using *ear,* write the word that matches the picture. You may look back.

1.		_____
2.		_____
3.		_____
4.		_____
5.		_____
6.		_____
7.		_____

Lesson 12

Sometimes *ear* says /er/, as in <u>ear</u>th.

Circle the word that matches the picture.

1.	sear seethe serve search	2.	elderly early easily eerie
3.	pear peal peer pearl	4.	earthquake earthworm earmark earring
5.	seasickness second-class searchlight sterling	6.	yearn yarn year yawn
7.	health earl earth equal	8.	learner leaner lantern leave
9.	hardly heard hurt horse	10.	egg eat ear earn

89

Circle the letters, and write the word that matches the picture.

1.		Spell.				Write.
		h g	ear ea	d b		_____
2.						
		ear ai	th ch			_____
3.						
		s z	ee ear	gh ch		_____
4.						
		p b	ea oa	m r		_____
5.						
		y l	ear or	m n		_____
6.						
		p b	ear ar	l t		_____
7.						
		or ear	m n	ing th		_____

Join the syllables to make a word that fits each meaning.
Use your dictionary to help you.

1.	worm quake earth	A shaking or trembling of the ground _____ A worm that helps loosen the soil _____
2.	light twi search	A device that can throw a powerful beam of light _____ The time of day between sunset and darkness _____
3.	earn ings feel	Money earned; wages _____ What gets hurt when someone is unkind _____ _____
4.	heard un earth	To dig up from the ground _____ Not heard _____
5.	ing search learn	Gaining knowledge or skill in something _____ Trying to find something by looking _____
6.	ware hard earthen	Objects made of baked clay; pottery _____ Tools made of metal _____
7.	hearse peat re	To practice for a show or play on stage _____ To say or do again _____

Yes or no?

	Yes	No
1. Could an earthquake ruin a house?	☐	☐
2. Do you like to go to bed earlier than midnight?	☐	☐
3. Would you search for a pearl in an oyster shell?	☐	☐
4. Can you earn money shoveling snow off sidewalks?	☐	☐
5. Would you search for an earthworm in your gravy?	☐	☐
6. Have you ever heard a nightingale sing "The Star-Spangled Banner"?	☐	☐
7. Would you look for your lost slipper with a searchlight?	☐	☐

Pick the best word to finish each sentence.

earliest	rehearsal	earthworms
yearning	earning	learn
searchlight	earthquake	earnestness

1. Before putting on the play, they had one last _____.

2. At night we dig in the garden for _____ to use as bait for fishing.

3. In the fog we could see the airport's _____ showing us where to land.

4. Serena got to the classroom as the sun was coming up; she was the student who arrived _____.

5. When the ground shook and the windows rattled, we knew there had been an _____.

6. Leroy is working at the supermarket where he is _____ eight dollars an hour.

7. I am trying to teach Rover to sit, roll over, and fetch a ball, but he is slow to _____.

Put an X after the sentence that matches the picture.

1. Kimberly always wears a pearl necklace when she gets dressed up. ☐

   Kimberly has a pear-shaped diamond ring on her finger. ☐

2. Donna learns to check the battery, to change the oil, and to pump gas. ☐

   Donna earns lots of money mowing grass and weeding gardens. ☐

3. The earthworm beckons to the nearsighted bird. ☐

   The early bird nearly always catches the earthworm. ☐

4. Earl produced a huge, handsome earthenware bowl. ☐

   Earl formed a search party after the huge earthquake. ☐

5. Earl planted a row of Idaho potatoes in the soft earth. ☐

   Bruno, the basset hound, searched in the soft earth until he found his bone. ☐

6. Priscilla got up early to reheat the coffee and make pancakes for breakfast. ☐

   Priscilla got up early to rehearse her lines for the play. ☐

7. Alexander points to JulieAnne, who is wearing a lovely pearl necklace. ☐

   Alexander appoints JulieAnne to be the head of the Earth Day parade. ☐

94

The Earthquake Legend

Long, long ago there was a man named Wilburforce who was very, very strong and powerful. Wilburforce could do almost anything—pull up trees, juggle rocks, move mountains. But he had never been able to catch a fish. One day he decided to get some bait and try again. Now Wilburforce had heard that "the early bird catches the worm," so he set out to find himself an early bird. First he looked in all the nests; then he checked the bushes and fields. Next he took out his searchlight, for he had learned never to work without good light. Wilburforce searched everywhere for an early bird, but all his hard work failed. He could not find an early bird or a worm. Wilburforce finally became so angry that he had a temper tantrum and pounded the earth with his fists until it shook. It is said that this is how earthquakes came to be.

Answer the following questions. You may look back at the story.

1. What was Wilburforce like? _____

   _____

2. What had Wilburforce never been able to do? _____

   _____

3. What did he use to see better? _____

4. What kind of bird did he look for? _____

5. What did Wilburforce pound? _____

6. What did Wilburforce cause to happen? _____

Using *ear,* write the word that matches the picture. You may look back.

1. _____

2. _____

3. _____

4. _____

5. _____

6. _____

7. _____

Lesson 13

The letters *ph* say /f/, as in *photo*.

Circle the word that matches the picture.

1.
eleventh
elevator
electric
elephant

2.
rally
Ralph
rapid
ramp

3.
potato
phonics
photo
phone

4.
trombone
trophy
trolley
tropic

5.
dodging
dolphin
dollar
pamphlet

6.
televise
telescope
telephone
telegram

7.
gooseberry
gopher
goldfish
goldfinch

8.
grabby
graph
great
grape

9.
photograph
paragraph
phonograph
autograph

10.
a b c d e f g
h i j k l m n
o p q r s t
u v w x y z
album
elephant
alphabet
almanac

Circle the letters, and write the word that matches the picture.

#		Spell.				Write.
1.		gh auto	u gra	ph x		_____
2.		ph th	o e	ty to		_____
3.		d b	ol u	phin fo		_____
4.		tr th	o a	phy gy		_____
5.	a b c d e f g h i j k l m n o p q r s t u v w x y z	a al	few pha	bug bet		_____
6.		R ph	ai al	og ph		_____
7.		cr gr	u a	ph ss		_____

Join the syllables to make a word that fits each meaning.
Use your dictionary to help you.

1.	graph photo bar	A chart that shows information _____ _____ A picture made by a camera _____
2.	scope tele phone	An instrument used to talk with someone _____ An instrument used to make distant objects seem nearer _____
3.	dol lar phin	A playful sea animal _____ One hundred pennies _____
4.	graph auto para	A group of written sentences that belong together _____ One's name written in one's own handwriting _____
5.	or phan chard	A child with no living parents _____ A place where fruit trees grow _____
6.	y phon ed	Not real_____ Called _____
7.	bet ter alpha	Improved in health _____ A set of letters used in writing _____

Yes or no?

	Yes	No
1. Can an elephant talk on a telephone?	☐	☐
2. Does a dolphin wear pearls underwater?	☐	☐
3. Can you sing along with an autograph?	☐	☐
4. When you were two years old, could you read the alphabet?	☐	☐
5. Would you be afraid if you were visited by a dolphin?	☐	☐
6. Is a photograph smaller than a dump truck?	☐	☐
7. If you win a trophy, will you be thrilled?	☐	☐

Pick the best word to finish each sentence.

phonics	graph	phone
photograph	trophy	phony
alphabet	dolphin	elephant

1. A _____ is an intelligent and playful sea animal about five to eight feet long.

2. You use the twenty-six letters of the _____ to write words.

3. When the _____ rings, you pick it up and say, "Hello."

4. The circus _____ raised the tent with its strong trunk.

5. If you are the fastest swimmer in a race, you may win a _____.

6. We took a _____ of the waterfall so we could remember what it looked like.

7. We learn _____ to help us sound out words.

Put an X after the sentence that matches the picture.

1.	The silver dolphin won a trophy in the fishing contest. ☐ The boating party is hoping to see dolphins and a tuna. ☐	
2.	Philip went to sea on a phony pirate ship. ☐ The dolphins leap from the sea. ☐	
3.	Cristophene snaps a photo of the cute stuffed elephant. ☐ The elephant swings a fan back and forth to cool Cristophene. ☐	
4.	The class shows its paragraphs to the substitute teacher. ☐ The teacher shows the class a graph of its progress. ☐	
5.	Philip is talking about Ralph's present on the telephone. ☐ Philip is taking a telescope to Rhonda so she can study the stars. ☐	
6.	Joseph twists the photograph into a funnel shape. ☐ Joseph does the twist while he plays the saxophone. ☐	
7.	The wallpaper has gophers and elephants painted on it. ☐ The gopher is carefully printing the alphabet on the chalkboard. ☐	

Student Gifts

Mr. Castle was talking to a group on Parents Night. He said, "My students—your kids—have gifts to give to our classroom community. Let me tell you about three students as examples.

"Phil takes photographs for hours with his phone. He won a trophy for a photo of some elephants that he saw on a trip to the zoo.

"Joseph loves to write. He knew the alphabet at age three and wrote perfect paragraphs by the age of nine. Now his fellow students ask for his autograph because they think he'll become a famous author!

"Sophie is a great math student. She gathers facts about the members of the class. She graphs the streets they live on, what they like to wear, and their favorite foods. Other students helped her decorate the graphs you see all around you.

"Let's honor all members of our class on this Parents Night!"

Answer the following questions. You may look back at the story.

1. Why are the parents at school? _____

2. What does Mr. Castle think about his students? _____

_____

3. What is Phil's gift? Joseph's gift? Sophie's gift? _____

_____

4. What do you think the parents did after Mr. Castle asked them to

honor the students? _____

5. Do you think Mr. Castle is a good teacher? Why? _____

_____

Using *ph*, write the word that matches the picture. You may look back.

1.		_____
2.		_____
3.		_____
4.	a b c d e f g h i j k l m n o p q r s t u v w x y z	_____
5.		_____
6.		_____
7.		_____

Lesson 14

The letters *ei* and *eigh* say /ā/, as in <u>eigh</u>t.

Circle the word that matches the picture.

1.	sigh slight sleigh share	2.	nighthawk newborn neighbor nightmare
3.	eighty eighteen arrow elegant	4.	rainfall reindeer reins ranger
5.	freight train freezer fainting frightening	6.	weightless makeshift waitress weight lifting
7.	vein veal veil vile	8.	wrap reins rates roof
9.	write rainy weigh await	10.	eighty-eight eighteen weighty eighty

Circle the letters, and write the word that matches the picture.

	Spell.			Write.
1.	w m	eigh ee	t p	_____
2.	eigh ea	t ck		_____
3.	sl sp	ow eigh		_____
4.	eigh ee	ry ty		_____
5.	w v	ei o	l t	_____
6.	br fr	igh eigh	d t	_____
7.	at eigh	ten teen		_____

Join the syllables to make a word that fits each meaning.
Use your dictionary to help you.

1.
deer	An animal with antlers _____
skin	A soft leather made from an animal skin
rein	_____

2.
eigh	
ty	Ten times eight equals _____
teen	Nine plus nine equals _____

3.
hood	
neighbor	A place where people live _____
child	The time when one is a child _____

4.
bells	Bells tied around a cow's neck so you can find it
cow	_____
sleigh	Bells on the harness of a horse drawing a sleigh
	_____

5.
un	
veil	To take off a veil or reveal _____
fair	Not just; not fair _____

6.
alls	
weight	Having too much weight _____
over	Loose pants with a bib and straps_____

7.
weight	
under	Weighing too little _____
ground	Beneath the surface of the earth _____

Yes or no?

		Yes	No
1.	Does a reindeer take a trolley car to work each day?	☐	☐
2.	Do you weigh as much as a freight train?	☐	☐
3.	Do a person's veins help the blood circulate?	☐	☐
4.	Do you want to join the army when you are eighteen years old?	☐	☐
5.	If you were a strong weight lifter, would you be able to lift a skyscraper?	☐	☐
6.	If your horse starts to run too fast, should you pull back on the reins?	☐	☐
7.	Would you ask your neighbor to prepare supper for you every night?	☐	☐

Pick the best word to finish each sentence.

eighty-eight	neighborhood	reindeer
freight train	overweight	sleighbells
unveil	weightlessness	eighteen

1. The _____ jingle as we glide over the snow-covered fields in our horse-drawn sleigh.

2. On Saturday afternoon, all the children in the _____ gather outside and play together.

3. Irving's grandfather is very old; he is _____ years old today.

4. Astronauts in outer space have a feeling of _____.

5. My package was _____ so I had to pay extra money to mail it.

6. The cart was pulled by eight _____.

7. You will be able to vote when you are _____ years old.

Put an X after the sentence that matches the picture.

1.	Charlie is not allowed to take photographs of the old masters. ☐ Charlie weighs a great deal more than his master. ☐	
2.	Neema is celebrating her eighteenth birthday. ☐ Eighty miles per hour is too fast, even for Neema's racing car. ☐	
3.	The large sleigh is packed full of ice-cream cones and other goodies. ☐ Since John stopped eating ice cream, he lost weight and can run in the race. ☐	
4.	Veronica pulls the long white veil off the new statue of the president. ☐ Veronica was wearing a lovely veil when she plunged off the diving board. ☐	
5.	Eartha cut the garbage up for coleslaw and put it in an earthenware bowl. ☐ Where on earth did the boy get that giant cabbage? ☐	
6.	The freight train is carrying eighty elephants to the circus. ☐ The elephants are training the reindeer to jump on the circus train. ☐	
7.	Phyllis did not want to ride the reindeer. ☐ The horse's reins were in Phil's hands. ☐	

110

Reindeer

Maybe you have seen reindeer at a zoo or a farm. But do you know where they come from?

Reindeer live in cold climates, close to the Arctic Circle. Males weigh about four hundred pounds, while females weigh about two hundred. Both males and females have antlers, but male antlers are much larger.

Reindeer are found in Norway and its neighbors Sweden and Finland. A tribe called the Sami herds the reindeer and uses them for meat, milk, and hides, as well as for hauling freight. Long ago, the Sami would walk or ski next to their reindeer herds. Now they follow them on snowmobiles.

Reindeer graze on moss, sedges, and grasses. In Norway, there are eighty-nine areas where reindeer can graze. Each Sami tribesman and his herd have two areas: a summer one and a winter one.

If you visit Finland, you can take a reindeer sleigh ride. After you watch the driver harness the reindeer, you ride into the forest to a wooden hut and campfire for some tea or coffee. Maybe the sleigh driver will let you hold the reins!

Answer the following questions. You may look back at the story.

1. Where do reindeer live? _____

2. How much do reindeer weigh? _____

3. What do the Sami use reindeer for? _____

4. How did the Sami follow their herds long ago? Now? _____

_____

5. Where can you go on a reindeer sleigh ride? _____

_____

Using *ei* the *eigh*, write the word that matches the picture. You may look back.

1.		_____
2.		_____
3.		_____
4.		_____
5.		_____
6.		_____
7.		_____

Lesson 15 • Review Lesson

Circle the word that matches the picture.

1.
wrapper
wrecker
writing
wringer

2.
kneeling
knee socks
knee cap
knocking

3.
overthrow
overhead
overwork
overweight

4.
chancing
charging
changing
chatting

5.
billion
billboard
building
bullfrog

6.
connect
concert
concrete
cornmeal

7.
notebook
knothole
nostril
knuckle

8.
faulty
faucet
fasten
father

9.
thumbnail
thumper
thunderbolt
thousand

10.
bombard
bandaged
banner
bankrupt

Circle the letters, and write the word that matches the picture.

		Spell.		Write.
1.		wri wro	tish ting	_____
2.		sneigh sneak	ress ers	_____
3.		knit knot	hole hold	_____
4.		bull bell	frog full	_____
5.		fay fau	scat cet	_____
6.		ever over	weight white	_____
7.		seat seed	bolt belt	_____

Join the syllables to make a word that fits each meaning.
Use your dictionary to help you.

1.	ter tipede cen	The middle point _____ A small wormlike animal with many legs _____
2.	ear ring phone	Part of a headset _____ A small ornament worn on the ear _____
3.	tic gigan at	A space or room just below the roof in a house _____ Huge; like a giant _____
4.	sau pas sage	A spicy ground meat _____ A path or tunnel _____
5.	ment ce equip	Furnishings; supplies _____ Substance used to hold bricks together _____
6.	bage cab gar	A vegetable with thick leaves that form a head _____ Scraps of food to be thrown away _____
7.	space friend ship	A craft used to travel to outer space _____ Being good pals _____

Yes or no?

	Yes	No
1. Would a squirrel wear fancy ruby earrings?	☐	☐
2. Would you keep your racehorse in a nice, cool cellar?	☐	☐
3. Can you squirt a seagull with the outside faucet?	☐	☐
4. Can you write to your senator about a problem?	☐	☐
5. Do you put the milk for your cereal into a saucer?	☐	☐
6. If your luggage is overweight, will the pilot throw it off the airplane?	☐	☐
7. Could you carry a billboard in your pocket?	☐	☐

Pick the best word to finish each sentence.

writing	overweight	faucet
neighborhood	billboard	squirrel
overheard	fierce	knives

1. I saw the _____ for the new shopping center.

2. Spongecake, the elephant, is _____ and must go on a diet.

3. Rodwick Rodgers is _____ a new book about an eighteenth-century shipwreck.

4. If you hear "drip-drip-drip" in the kitchen, you probably have a leaky _____.

5. That police guard dog looks very wild and _____.

6. Yesterday I _____ my teacher say that we were going to have a surprise quiz today.

7. We set the table with plates, glasses, forks, _____, and spoons.

Put an X after the sentence that matches the picture.

1. Up north, reindeer pull sleighs over the snowy winter landscape. ☐

   John Johnson came in eighth in a ten-speed bike race. ☐

2. The dogs and cats in our neighborhood do not seem to bother the catbirds. ☐

   We have eighteen dogs and eight cats in our neighborhood. ☐

3. The lovely bride wears a lacy gown and an eighteen-foot veil. ☐

   Bridget's lovely bonnet has bird feathers and a silk veil. ☐

4. Alvin was so worried that he bit his thumbnails way down. ☐

   The hammer hit Alvin's thumb instead of the nail. ☐

5. The frying pan weighed much more than the saucepan. ☐

   The overweight sausage danced around the frying pan. ☐

6. The foxy hound has the know-how to escape its kennel. ☐

   The twin sisters are taking charge of the fox hound. ☐

7. We watch the game through a gigantic knothole in the fence. ☐

   Reevon peeks through the keyhole of the trunk full of jewels. ☐

Can Phil Fix His Faucet?

After work one day, Phil relaxed into his lounge chair. He tried to listen to some music, but the drip, drip, drip of the kitchen faucet was too distracting. He asked himself, "Should I phone my neighbor George? He's a plumber, but they charge too much!"

Phil decided to fix his own faucet. First he unfastened the faucet cap and stuck his finger up the pipe. He could feel the skin on his knuckle tear. "I'll just bandage that," he thought. Next Phil stuck a bent coat hanger up the faucet pipe, and this time he scraped his thumb and his wrist. More bandages.

After eight more unsuccessful tries, Phil knew he had been wrong. He needed a plumber. Just then Phil saw George out walking his dog. He opened the kitchen window, leaned out onto the ledge, and cried, "Help! My faucet's dripping, and I'm out of bandages!"

"Honestly, Phil," said George, looking up at his neighbor. "Why didn't you ask? You know that for neighbors, there is no charge!"

Answer the following questions. You may look back at the story.

1. How did Phil try to relax after work? _____

2. What was bothering Phil? _____

3. Why didn't Phil call George right away? _____

_____

4. Which parts of his body did Phil bandage? _____

_____

5. Did George know why Phil never asked for help before? What makes you think so? _____

In the crossword puzzle below, read each clue and write the word in the boxes. Remember that some words go across, and some words go down.

ACROSS

2. What happens when two things (like cars) collide
4. Goods and cargo carried by train, ship, or airplane
6. Recommendation or information given about what should be done
8. To do something over and over to learn it; to drill
10. To write one's name on a book or photo
11. A polite, well-mannered man
12. The joint between your hand and your arm
13. A contest of speed (as in running or sailing)
15. Not dry
16. Tied in knots
17. The plural of mouse

DOWN

1. The highest officer in the United States Army
3. A person who commands others in an army or navy
5. Sixty minutes make one _____
7. Truthful
8. A device used to call and talk to people
9. To have a party on some special occasion
11. Kind, tender, soft
14. The opposite of begin

Book 7 — Posttest

Circle the word that matches the meaning.

1. A bit of bread or toast crab comb crumb crump	2. One who tends sheep shipper shilling sheriff shepherd
3. The joint between the hand and arm wrestle wrist rest worst	4. Trustworthy hornet hottest honey honest
5. The home of a king or queen place policy pace palace	6. A baby sheep lame last lamp lamb
7. Something odd or peculiar strangle strange stage struggle	8. To promise plug pledge plead plunge
9. A pull or handle on a chest knob knot knock knack	10. What people do when music is played lessen listed listen litter

In each group of syllables below, circle the three that will join to make a word. Write the word on the line. If no word can be found, write "no word."

1. (mem) (re) act (ber) _remember_	2. pres ly ing or _no word_
3. ber cem De web _____	4. to ast graph pho _____
5. brate cel tine e _____	6. neigh est hood bor _____
7. ber cum cu ang _____	8. wres no gate ten _____
9. gym rand nas tic _____	10. gan gi tic ben _____
11. ger knit ho pen _____	12. ty mes ger sen _____

Use the picture clues to fill the blanks.

Phil had a new black Labrador puppy named Duke who came running

whenever Phil _____. But Phil also had a problem.

Duke was beginning to teethe, and his baby teeth were like steel.

Duke began by nibbling Phil's _____.

Then he chewed up a nice _____ as well

as a _____ of Phil's parents. Next, he

gnawed on Phil's best sneakers, the edge of the living room carpet,

and even the backyard _____. Phil worked

hard to _____ a present for a neighbor. It

seemed like the last straw when Duke _____

on the table and chewed it up.

One day Phil came in the _____ and saw Duke

on the floor moaning. The end of the ball of _____

was coming out of his mouth. Phil and Dad took Duke to the vet. A few

days and 80 _____ dollars later, Duke was fine again.

Read the story and answer the questions.

The Hero

Poor John had run for club president twice and been defeated. "I guess I should run for something else," he said. "I'll run in a marathon race instead."

Now John was in good shape. He was not overweight, and he jogged ten miles every day. But John was no teenager; he was seventy-eight years old!

The morning of the race all the runners were at the starting gate stretching, registering with the judges, and selecting numbered tee shirts. John was number eighty-eight. Finally the whistle blew, and the runners set off.

In a long-distance race, it is important not to run too fast, but to pace yourself. You should always breathe through your mouth and never look down at the ground.

The distance of this race was twenty-six miles. Slowly the younger runners pulled ahead of John. He was tired but he kept plodding along. When he became too warm, he threw off his sweatshirt. Once, a person ran along beside him and offered him some water from a canteen. On John went, but no one else was any longer in sight!

At last, knees knocking and heart pounding, he saw the finish line. The others had crossed it long ago. But as John fell panting over the finish line, photos snapped and excited people cheered. The judges wrote down his time. John had finished last, but he got more cheers than the winner. Keep on trucking, John!

1. Why was John a hero? _____

2. How did John keep in shape? _____

3. What is one rule to remember in long-distance racing?

   _____

4. What was John's reward? _____

   _____